Unforgettable Jokes, Quotes And Trivia

Hours Of
Enjoyable Reading

Sidney Scott Clarkson

Fairway Press
Lima, Ohio

FIRST EDITION
Copyright © 1994 by
Sidney Scott Clarkson

———————

Library of Congress Catalog Card Number: 94-72254

———————

ISBN 1-55673-950-8   PRINTED IN U.S.A.

This book is dedicated to the greatest gift God has given me, my two children Austin and Nadine Clarkson.

Humorous Stories

And

Jokes

This book is a treasure trove of things everybody should know but doesn't. If you memorize all this stuff you'll be the most interesting person alive.
— Phyllis Diller
Entertainer and Comedienne

THE geography of Ohio: round on the sides and high in the middle.

MY aunt really has a terrible weight problem: She can't wait to eat.

I got in an argument with a gang in a dark alley. I said, "Hold it, I've got a black belt." They just started laughing until I said, "With a '.45' in it."

A girl was kicking on my door at four a.m. I had to get up and let her out.

MY dad is with the FBI. They caught him in Detroit.

MY town is so small that the local prostitute is a virgin.

WE were so poor when I was young that we could not afford a dog. When we saw a burglar we had to bark ourselves.

WE were so poor we'd just walk past a bank and the alarms would go off.

YOU know your town is small when there are more combines than cars.

MY dad ate so much that when he went to a restaurant he didn't bother getting a menu, he got an estimate.

MIXED emotions is when your mother-in-law goes over a cliff in your new Cadillac.

YOU know your town is small when you don't need to use turn signals. Everybody knows where you're going anyway.

MIXED emotions is when your daughter comes back from a date with a Gideon Bible.

SPRING has sprung, Fall has fell, Winter is here and it feels like hell.

I got a new job during college. My employer said he would pay me weekly. I received my first check and thought that my employer was right, he did pay weakly.

MY doctor told me I should watch my weight. So I got it out here where I can see it.

A man was talking to his girlfriend. He wanted to tell her that when he was with her it seemed like time stood still. He got nervous and said, "Your face would stop a clock." Then he wanted to tell her she was open-minded. He got nervous again and said, "You have a hole in your head."

A man was scurrying through the want ads for he needed a job badly. He had been unemployed for five months and had a wife and four children. He finally saw an ad at the city zoo. He went immediately to see the zookeeper. The zookeeper greeted him and explained the job. "You see, our gorilla died and we need someone to dress in this gorilla suit and keep our patrons happy until our real one comes back." The man thought about it a couple of days and in need came back to accept. He got in the cage and the patrons immediately loved him. So in order not to lose his job when the real gorilla came back, he wanted to do something spectacular. He got on the tire and started swinging back and forth. People started cheering and throwing apples and oranges. Suddenly, the tire broke and he went sailing into the lion's cage. He started running around and screaming, "Help, help! Get me out of here!" The lion came up to him and said, "Hey buddy, shut up before we all get fired."

A judge was giving the verdict on a divorce case in the court. The separated couple was standing before the judge. The judge began, "I'm going to give your wife $50 a week." "Well, gee," said the man, "that's awfully nice of you. I'll even throw in a dollar."

Money

WORKERS earn it
Spendthrifts burn it
Bankers lend it
Women spend it
Forgers fake it
Taxes take it
Dying leaves it
Heirs receive it
Thrifty save it
Misers crave it
Robbers seize it
Rich increase it
Gamblers lose it
I could use it

Suicide

RAZORS pain you
Rivers are damp,
Acids stain you
And drugs cause cramp,
Guns aren't lawful
Nooses give,
Gas smells awful
You might as well live.

Liquor And Living Long

THE horse and mule live 30 years
And know nothing of wines and beers.
The goat and sheep at 20 die
And never a taste of scotch or rye.
The cow drinks water by the ton
And at 18 is mostly done.
The dog at 15 cashes in
Without the aid of rum or gin.
The cat in milk and water soaks
And then in 12 short years it croaks.
The modest, sober, bone-dry hen
Lays eggs for feed, then dies at ten.
All animals are strictly dry:
They sinless live and swiftly die;
But sinful, ginful, rum-soaked men
Survive for three score years and ten.
And some of them, a very few,
Stay pickled 'til they're 92.

The Gorilla

THE sacred ape, now, children, see
He's searching for the modest flea
If he should turn around we'd find
He has no hair on his behind.

I was often taught in my speech classes in college the ABC's of speaking. However one also must not forget the XYZ's: Examine Your Zipper.

A woman won the lottery and immediately called home to tell her husband. "Hurry, I just won the lottery. Quickly pack your suitcase." "That's great," he replied. "Summer or winter clothes?" "All of them. I want you out by six."

TO encourage his teenage son to cut the lawn, the father got a belt-driven lawnmower. He took off his belt and the son started pushing the lawnmower.

ONE day a customer walked into a pet shop and asked the clerk for a mouse and 20 cockroaches. Puzzled, the clerk asked the reason for such a purchase. "Well," replied the man, "I'm moving out of my apartment and the landlord asked me to leave the apartment in the same condition I found it."

A reporter asked Bill Clinton, "Mr. President, what do you think about the abortion bill?" "Hillary paid it," remarked Clinton.

AFTER a preacher died and went to heaven, he noticed a New York cab driver had been given a higher place than he. "I don't understand, Saint Peter. I have devoted my entire life to service." "Our policy is to reward results. Now what happened to you whenever you gave a sermon?" asked Saint Peter. The minister admitted that many members of the congregation fell asleep. "And what happened when people rode in this man's taxi? They not only stayed awake, they prayed."

DURING a press conference a reporter asked Reagan, "Mr. President, how are your Soviet relations?" "How should I know?" replied Reagan. "I have no relation in the Soviet Union; my mother never got out of Illinois." Another reporter asked, "Mr. President, what kind of water do you like?" "Well," replied Reagan.

AN American and Russian were talking one day and the American said, "You know, here in the U.S. I can go to Washington, D.C., go right up Pennsylvania Ave., walk in the Oval Office, pound on Bill Clinton's desk and say, 'I don't like the way you're running this country!' " The Russian replied, "I can do that." "You can?" said the American in a puzzled manner. "Yes," said the Russian, "I can go to Moscow, march into the Kremlin, go into Yeltsin's office and pound on his desk and say, 'I don't like the way President Clinton is running his country!' "

A German brigade was holding an English paratrooper captive. They were torturing him. The English soldier said, "Please cut off my right leg and drop it over Mother England." They came back a week later and the Englishman asked, "Please just take my left leg and drop it over Mother England." It got down to the point where the English soldier only had his left arm attached. The Germans came back to torture him again. The soldier asked, "Please take my left arm and drop it over Mother England." "Nein," said the German soldiers, "we can't do that anymore. We think you're trying to escape."

A man worrying about the draft confided in a friend. His older friend said, "Well, if you get drafted you've got two options: active duty or non-active duty. If you get on non-active you've got nothing to worry about. And if you do get on active duty you still have two options. You can be sent overseas or be stationed at home. If you get stationed at home you've got nothing to worry about, and if you get sent overseas you still have two options: you can be put at the front of the lines or the back. Now if you get put in the back of the lines, you have nothing to worry about; but if you get put in front of the lines, you still have two options: you can be hit or not hit. Now if you don't get hit, you've got nothing to worry about, but if you get hit you've still got two options. It can be fatal or it can be not fatal. If it's fatal, you still have two options.

Impeccable Quotes

IF you stand for nothing, you will fall for anything.

ROMANCE without finance becomes a nuisance.

SOMEONE told me that success is not knowing that you cannot do something.

IT is said you go far by just being yourself.

GENIUS is 1% inspiration and 99% perspiration.
— Thomas Edison

LUCK is the residue of design.

IF you fail to plan, you plan to fail.

THERE is no better relief than doing what is right.

BAD politicians are elected by good people who don't vote.

SOMETIMES a run of bad luck is just what a fellow needs to get smart.

HE who asks a question is a fool for five minutes. He who does not ask a question remains a fool forever.

WHERE there is smoke, there is often no fire — just a smoke-making machine.
— John F. Kennedy

FLATTERY will get you everywhere.

IT takes a lot of work to get to the top and even more to stay there.

WITH God, all things are possible.

WHAT the mind can conceive can be achieved.

POLITICS is like war but only worse; in war you only get defeated once.
— Winston Churchill

SOMEBODY should tell us, right at the start of our lives, that we are dying. Then we might live life to the limit. Every minute of every day, do it! I say — whatever you want to do, do it now! There are only so many tomorrows.
— Michael Landon, shortly before he died of cancer

EVERYONE on this earth has an appointment with death. Live as though your appointment will come this year.

A person, in the end, will be known more for his action, not his knowledge. Enthusiasm and perseverance can be more helpful than knowledge and wisdom.

A good teacher tells,
A great teacher explains,
A terrific teacher demonstrates,
An excellent teacher inspires.

YOU never fail if you keep on keeping on.

JUDGE not, that ye be not judged.

NOTHING is good or bad, but thinking makes it so.

— Shakespeare

THE royal road to a man's heart is to talk to him about things he treasures most.

LEADERS are not born, they are made. And they are made just like anything else that has ever been made in this country — by hard work. And that is the price that we have to pay to achieve that goal.

— Vince Lombardi

MONEY doesn't change people; it only exaggerates what is already there.

A dollar saved is an oversight by Congress.

ALL laws are simply guidelines for being nice to each other.

WOMEN are like tea bags: You don't know their strength until they are in hot water.

Don't Be Afraid To Fail

YOU'VE failed many times, although you may not remember.

You fell down the first time you tried to walk.

You almost drowned the first time you tried to swim, didn't you?

Did you hit the ball the first time you swung?

Heavy hitters, the ones who hit the most home runs, also strike out a lot.

R. H. Macy failed seven times before his store, in New York, caught on.

English novelist, John C. Easey, got 753 rejection slips before he published 564 books.

Babe Ruth struck out 1,330 times, but he also hit 714 home runs.

Don't worry about failure, but worry about the chances you miss when you don't even try.

PEOPLE think about 50,000 thoughts a day.
You should make these thoughts positive.
What you think is what you will get to.

I am not bound to win, but I am bound to be true.
I am not bound to succeed, but I am bound to live up to what light I have.
I must stand with anybody that stands right.
I stand with him while he is right, and part with him when he goes wrong.
— Abraham Lincoln

A leader doesn't worry about being on the right track, he makes the track.

TIME is the biggest glutton of life.

ONE day, the sun and the wind quarreled about who was stronger. The wind said, "See that old man down there with a coat? I bet I can make him take his coat off quicker than you can."

So the sun went behind a cloud and the wind blew until it was almost a tornado; but the harder it blew, the tighter the old man wrapped his coat about him.

Finally, the wind calmed down and gave up. Then the sun came out and smiled a ray of sunshine on the old man. The man wiped his brow and shed the coat.

The sun told the wind that gentleness and friendliness were always stronger than fury and force.

YOU cannot bring about prosperity by discouraging thrift.
You cannot help small men by tearing down big men.
You cannot strengthen the weak by weakening the strong.
You cannot lift the wage earner by pulling down the wage payer.
You cannot help the poor man by destroying the rich.
You cannot keep out of trouble by spending more than your income.
You cannot further the brotherhood of man by inciting class hatred.
You cannot build character and courage by taking away man's initiative and
        independence.
You cannot help men permanently, by doing what they could and should do.
— Abraham Lincoln

THE dogmas of the quiet past are inadequate for the stormy present. The occasion is piled high with difficulty and we must rise to the occasion, as our case is new, so we must think anew and act anew.

— Abraham Lincoln, State of the Union message, December 1862

SUCCESS and failure can have much in common that is good, if, during both, you tried.

IF you aim at nothing, you will hit it every time.

IF you like sausage for breakfast and have respect for the law, never watch either being made.

To Achieve Your Dreams, Remember Your ABC's

Avoid negative sources, people, places, things and habits.

Believe in yourself.

Consider things from every angle.

Don't give up, and don't give in.

Enjoy life today; yesterday is gone and tomorrow may never come.

Family and friends are hidden treasures; enjoy their riches.

Give more than you planned to give.

Hang on to your dreams.

Ignore those who try to discourage you.

Just do it!

Keep trying — no matter how hard it seems, it will get easier.

Love yourself first and most.

Make it happen.

Never lie, cheat or steal. Always strike a fair deal.

Open your eyes, and see things as they really are.

Practice makes perfect.

Quitters never win and winners never quit.

Read, study and learn about everything important in your life.

Stop procrastinating.

Take control of your own destiny.

Understand yourself in order to understand others better.

Visualize it.

Want it more than anything.

Xccelerate your efforts.

You are unique of all of God's creations; nothing can replace you.

Zero in on your target and go for it!

THE power inside of us all is electricity — make it work in a positive way. It is like an outlet: Put your finger in it and get shocked; plug in your radio and get beautiful music for your effort.

IN life you never stay the same: You either recede or go forward.

ONE can feel at times like a spinning leaf blown along a dirty street; one can feel like a grain of sand stuck in one place. But nobody has said that life was a calm and orderly thing; it isn't. One isn't a tattered leaf nor a grain of sand; one can, to a greater or lesser degree, draw his road map and follow.

FRIENDSHIPS seldom last except between equals.

WHAT you give you receive. Since action and reaction are equal, you keep what you give away. You will be enriched by giving of yourself, not by giving with expectation of return.

FOOTBALL games are won at the line of scrimmage, wars are won on the battlefield, and elections are won at the grassroots level.

— Scott Clarkson

HATRED is never ended by hatred but by love.

— Buddha

BY fighting you never get enough, but by yielding you get more than you expected.

EVEN victory must be tempered with caution.

Presidential

Trivia

THE only President to be inaugurated by his father was Calvin Coolidge in 1923, shortly after the unexpected death of Warren G. Harding. Coolidge was awakened by his father, who administered the oath. After it was given, Coolidge, now the 30th President of the United States, went back to bed for a few more hours of sleep.

PRESIDENT Reagan consumed jellybeans as a substitute for his habit of smoking. These were not the regular over-the-counter jellybeans but ones made with natural flavorings.

IN the 1960 television debates between Kennedy and Nixon, Rose Kennedy, John Kennedy's mother, said her son looked and sounded like young Lincoln. Mrs. Nixon on the other hand, telephoned her son to ask if anything was wrong because he did not look well.

THE youngest president ever elected to the office was John Kennedy (43). The youngest person ever to be president was Theodore Roosevelt (42). The youngest person ever to be vice-president was Richard Nixon under President Eisenhower. The oldest person to be vice-president was Alben Barkley under President Truman.

CHOOSING Lyndon Johnson as a vice-presidential running mate did not please a lot of Kennedy supporters. Kennedy however saw the advantages of picking a Southern Democrat. He also thought Johnson would not accept. When John went to inform his younger brother Bobby that Johnson had indeed accepted, Bobby's reaction was "Oh my God, now what do we do?"

GROVER Cleveland dated an unattached widow named Maria Crofts Halpin. She lived with her two children not far from Grover's apartment in Buffalo, New York. Because of their intimacy, they discovered that she was to have a child. Grover never chose to marry her but arranged for her and her children to be taken care of. On June 2, 1886, President Cleveland, then 49 years old, married Frances Folsom, who was 28 years younger than Grover. They took their wedding vows inside the White House.

DURING the Civil War Dan Rice was the country's most popular clown. He owned his own circus and traveled up and down the major rivers performing. He is the only clown in American history ever to be asked to run for president.

WHEN asked for advice on John Kennedy's campaign for Congress, his newly hired campaign advisor remarked, "It takes three things to win a campaign. The first thing is money, the second thing is money, and the third thing is money."

— Joe Kane, political advisor to John Kennedy

OUR shortest president was James Madison at 5 feet 2 inches. Our tallest president was Lincoln at 6 feet 4 inches. Our heaviest president was William Taft who at one time weighed 300 pounds. Since he was so heavy President Taft's size was a subject of national humor. The president never let this stop him from one of his favorite leisure activities, dancing. He would often spend evenings on the White House patio along with his wife and their favorite records. Taft's bathtub, specially made, was able to hold four people.

THE shortest term in office for a president was that of William Henry Harrison who died of pneumonia at the age of 68, serving only one month. The next shortest term was that of James Garfield who served five and a half months until he died of an assassin's bullet in 1881.

PRESIDENT McKinley's wife was an epileptic. This never stopped her however from escorting her husband to every social event he attended. Frequently when she would have a seizure McKinley would pull out his handkerchief, cover her mouth and guide her to the next nearest room while excusing himself from the embarrassed guest.

CAMPAIGNING for the presidency in 1896, Democratic candidate William Jennings Bryan went around the country to sound his message. On the other hand, Republican candidate William McKinley never left his home in Canton, Ohio. He campaigned from his front porch giving speeches to the trainloads of people that arrived daily.

THEODORE Roosevelt was a great admirer and participant in many sporting events. While in the White House he would occasionally bring in boxers and spar with them. During one match, the president took a blow to the head that consequently blinded his left eye. This was a very well kept secret in the White House.

AT the Pan-American exposition in Buffalo, New York, on September 6, 1901, President McKinley was to give another speech. The doors of the Temple of Music Building closed at 4:07 after hundreds of people entered. Just then, a man named Leon Czolgosz approached the president and extended his arm to shake hands. Czolgosz raised his right hand which held a .32 caliber pistol concealed under a white handkerchief. He fired two shots into McKinley. The president fell backwards into the arms of a secret service agent. Police began to drag Czolgosz away and in doing so began to punch him. At seeing this, McKinley, his clothing drenched with blood, called out, "Don't let them hurt him."

OUR 30th President of the United States, Calvin Coolidge, sometimes called "Silent Cal," once said that he never got in trouble for anything he didn't say. One time at a dinner, a woman sat down beside him and said, "I made a bet that I could make you say more than two words." "You lose," replied Coolidge.

JOHN F. Kennedy smoked two cigars immediately after lunch on a daily basis.

TO curb his desire for a cigarette Ronald Reagan turned to eating jellybeans. Being an All-American man with common tastes, one of Reagan's all-time favorite foods is macaroni and cheese.

ONE of Abraham Lincoln's first jobs early in his career was being a postmaster in Illinois. Carrying letters around in his stovepipe hat, Lincoln would pass out letters as he would see their recipients on the street.

PRESIDENT Jimmy Carter's micro-management of the office was so exact to details that he personally would schedule the use of the White House tennis courts.

THE only president to be sworn in using his nickname was James Earl Carter. He took the oath of office using "Jimmy Carter" which he was commonly called.

THEODORE Roosevelt nearly banned the game of football in 1905 after 18 college players were killed and 159 badly injured while playing the game.

DURING WWI President Wilson, in order to save manpower and set a good example for the nation, had sheep "cut" the White House lawn.

BEING a very religious man Andrew Jackson wanted to die on a Sunday. His wish was answered. President Jackson died on Sunday, June 8, 1845.

THE president who had the most brothers and sisters was Benjamin Harrison with 12 siblings.

THESE three presidents were left-handed: Harry Truman, Gerald Ford, George Bush.

PRESIDENT George Bush stayed in touch with more than 4,000 friends through phone calls and letters during his tenure in the White House.

IN a fundraising baseball game for the Screen Actors Guild, Ronald Reagan badly twisted his ankle which has caused him to walk with a limp to this day.

THE first and only presidential home to be restored and made into a museum while the president was still alive was Ronald Reagan's in Dixon, Illinois.

ABRAHAM Lincoln offered General Lee the job of Commander of the Armed Forces of the Union Army. Lee detested slavery: He even freed his own slaves. But Lee, a Virginian, put state above nation.

ABRAHAM Lincoln chose honor over self-peace when he married Mary Todd. Their wedding date was set. Her father, being a wealthy man, hired a chef, had a dress made and bought a stove to cook the meal. At 12 noon the church was filled and the wedding ready to begin. However, Lincoln did not show up. They had to postpone the event until Lincoln got the courage to marry her.

IN 1863, when Abraham Lincoln's body lay in state in the Capitol's rotunda in Columbus, Ohio, the population of the city was only 15,000. However, 50,000 people came to show him respect.

AT age sixteen, George Washington was hired for a surveying expedition as a chainman. While sleeping outdoors for 17 nights, the men often slept on straw. One night near the end of the trip, the straw on which Washington was sleeping caught on fire. Fortunately, one of the men caught sight of the flames and extinguished it in time.

ABRAHAM Lincoln was never known for his tidiness. As a lawyer in Springfield, Illinois, his desk was a mess. It was so cluttered that he bundled a stack of papers and wrote, "When you can't find it anywhere else look here."

ON Lincoln's first day in the White House, office seekers overwhelmed him. One woman came to Lincoln and asked for a job for her husband saying he was too drunk to come. Soon after, Lincoln got smallpox and said to tell them all to come back for now he had something to give them all.

WHEN Harry Truman was a young man back in Independence, Missouri, he had a liking for a slender, blue-eyed girl named Bess who had a busy social life. Harry worked two jobs, one as a bank teller and the other on weekends as an usher at a movie theater. At one showing Bess showed up with a date. The theater was crowded and dark. Harry swiftly seated Bess in the tenth row and her date in the front row.

PRESIDENT Harry Truman, his wife and daughter, and a United States Senator were returning from Washington to Independence, Missouri. Passing through Hagerstown, Maryland, Truman ran straight through a stop sign. Another vehicle, not able to stop, hit their car causing it to strike a lamp post. The lamp post fell on top of the demolished vehicle. Mrs. Truman injured her neck. Their daughter had to be pulled out of the rear window, fortunately uninjured.

WHAT does every president from George Washington to George Bush have in common? They have all worn glasses.

CALVIN Coolidge's will consisted of one sentence.

PRESIDENT Eisenhower used to get a piece of string and place it on a table. He would then push it and say, "See, nothing happens." Then he would pull it and the string would travel smoothly. His point was that if leaders were to get people to follow they had to lead, not push.

DID the U.S. ever have a king as its ruler? Yes, Gerald King, who was adopted and his last name changed to Ford. Our current president was also adopted by his stepfather. His name was previously Bill Blythe.

THE White House during the presidency of Abraham Lincoln was so filled with visitors to see the president that Lincoln had to alter his policy of unlimited visiting hours. The hours were from 10 a.m. until 1 p.m. on Mondays, Wednesdays and Thursdays, and from 10 a.m. to 12 noon on Tuesdays and Fridays. Believe it not, virtually any citizen, if he waited long enough, could meet the President of the United States.

THE shortest inaugural address was delivered by George Washington. It was merely 135 words. William Henry Harrison gave the longest address. It was 9,000 words and took him two hours to deliver. He stood all this time in freezing temperatures and a northeast wind chilled him to the bone. The next day he came down with a cold. A month later he died of pneumonia.

PRESIDENT Adams, losing his second term to Thomas Jefferson, was so furious he refused to stand up at Jefferson's swearing in ceremony.

THEODORE Roosevelt made a personal commitment to himself that he would work as hard as he could until he turned 60. He fervently believed in a strenuous life. Unfortunately, he died at age 61.

THE 35th president of the U.S., John Kennedy, was sworn in January 20, 1961. The day before, Washington, D.C., was hit by one of the worst snow storms in the city's history. 550 snow plows and dump trucks were called upon to clear Pennsylvania Avenue for the parade. This was the first inauguration to have as many as five balls. President Kennedy attended every one. First Lady Jackie Kennedy attended the first two. However, Mrs. Kennedy became too fatigued to continue to the other balls.

DURING his presidency, Grover Cleveland developed cancer in his left upper jaw. A secret operation was arranged aboard a ship called the *Oneida* on the East River in New York. The operation was performed in a chair. Cleveland was given extra anesthesia. A large dose of nitrous oxide was needed since he weighed nearly 250 pounds and was a heavy beer drinker which causes a resistance to the anesthesia. Cocaine was also put on the inside of his mouth to numb the jaw before cutting it out. Not all of the cancer was removed. While operating, the doctors found that the cancer had spread around Cleveland's eye. Removing it would mean the president would be left with a sagging eye and double-vision.

JAMES Madison was restrained from entering the military because of his health. He served a brief spell as a minuteman only to drop out because of his lack of stamina. Madison constantly complained of high fevers, diarrhea and seizures much like those of an epileptic.

THOMAS Jefferson and James Madison both disliked Patrick Henry. While minister to France, Jefferson once wrote Madison saying that while Henry lived in America there would be little hope of reform and "what we have to do is devoutly pray for his death." The letters between the two took an average of seven weeks to reach one another.

FRANKLIN D. Roosevelt is the only president to ever marry a woman of the same last name, Eleanor Roosevelt. They were second cousins. The only president never to be married was James Buchanan. The first divorced president was Ronald Reagan.

IN 1952 Senator Richard Nixon, who was the Republican candidate for vice-president, had to give an explanation speech to tell about allegations that he was using campaign funds for personal uses. It was called his "Checkers speech" because he mentioned their cocker spaniel dog which was a gift to the family. In their hotel room in Cleveland, Ohio, Republican presidential candidate Dwight Eisenhower and his wife watched Nixon on television. Mamie Eisenhower found the speech so heartening that she started crying.

NIXON started his political career in 1945 running for Congress. He financed his campaign in part from poker winnings from his Navy days. During that campaign, Nixon's election office was broken into and his campaign materials were destroyed.

BEFORE Ronald Reagan was to have surgery to remove a bullet from his chest after he was shot, he looked up at the doctors and said, "I hope all of you are Republicans." Another time when he was being escorted through a building, the guide said, "Now go to the right." "Always," replied Reagan in his quick humor style.

RUTHERFORD B. Hayes, our twentieth president, escaped death numerous times throughout his career. In May of 1862, during a Civil War battle in West Virginia, Hayes was a leader of the Twenty-Third Regiment from Ohio. As the Confederates began to charge, a piece of shell fragment sliced Hayes' right knee. Again in September of that same year, Hayes led the Twenty-Third into battle in Maryland. A musket ball penetrated Hayes' left arm. Altogether, Hayes endured five bullet wounds during the war.

THEN in 1876 in Columbus, Ohio, where Hayes was Governor and running for the presidency, his life was once again endangered. Hayes was having dinner with his wife when suddenly a bullet burst through the window. Fortunately it missed Governor Hayes and went into the wall.

WHEN Theodore Roosevelt became president, the name of the president's mansion was changed to the White House. President Roosevelt would often bring in boxers to spar with. On one occasion he took a severe hit to the eye. He then started to bring in jujitsu wrestlers. On one occasion President Roosevelt had his secretary of war, William Howard Taft, a giant man of 300 pounds, wrestle a small Japanese instructor. Roosevelt watched in amusement as Taft was easily spun to the ground. Teddy Roosevelt was the first president to travel outside the U.S. while president (Panama). He is also the first president to fly in an airplane.

ON September 10, 1842, Letitia Tyler, wife of President John Tyler, died after never recovering from a stroke four years earlier. In 1844, President Tyler, at age 54, married Julia Garniner, age 24. They would have seven children together. In 1861, after serving as president, Tyler ran and won a seat in the Confederate Congress and went to Richmond, Virginia, for its first session. While he was staying at the Exchange Hotel, Mrs. Tyler had a dream that her husband was very ill and hurriedly rushed to her husband. Coincidentally, just a few days later, Tyler became ill and suddenly died. Ironically, 27 years later, Letitia Tyler died while staying at the Exchange Hotel in Richmond, Virginia.

BENJAMIN F. Tracey, Secretary of the Navy in President Harrison's administration had a tragic experience. One evening a house caught on fire. President Harrison saw the house on fire and rushed to the scene. When he arrived he performed artificial respiration on Secretary Tracey, saving his life. The president had him move into the White House until his recovery. Tracey's wife and daughter were killed in the fire.

DURING the election of 1889, Republican supporters of Benjamin Harrison rolled a 1,000 pound, red, white and blue ball that was 42 feet around into Indianapolis all the way from Maryland.

A man returning home to Cincinnati, Ohio, after the War of 1812, found his life much harder than when he had left. Two of his sons had piled up huge debts: John owed $12,000 and William owed $18,000 which was a huge amount of money in the 1800s. The father himself owed $20,000. He started paying off his sons' debts first by selling parts of his farm.

SIX months later his son, John, died of typhoid fever, leaving a wife and six children. So he took in his son's wife and six children. It soon became clear that his other son, William, Jr., was an alcoholic and could not provide for his family. The father took him and his family in too. The following spring, it rained so much that the Ohio River flooded his farm and all of his crops. He tried scheme after scheme to raise money for his family. Finally he became seriously ill. His friends were amazed at how cheerful he remained throughout these hard times. He soon got well and was offered a job as a clerk of courts with the Cincinnati Court of Common Pleas. Then in 1836, as he put it, "The strangest thing happened." He was approached by his party to run for President of the U.S. He got the nomination and was badly beaten. Still poor and with nothing to lose he ran again four years later and this time, William Henry Harrison became our 9th president.

General

Trivia

What animal has the most reports of taking human lives every year?
Shark

What is the biggest river in the world?   *Amazon*

What is the longest river in the world?   *Nile*

Who was our heaviest president?   *Taft*

How much did he weigh?   *300 pounds*

Who was our oldest president?   *Reagan*

Who was our youngest president?   *T. Roosevelt*

Who was our youngest elected president?   *J. F. Kennedy*

What is the world's strongest dog?   *Bull Mastiff*

What is the world's biggest dog?   *Saint Bernard*

What is the world's smallest dog?   *Chihuahua*

What is the world's tallest dog?   *Irish Wolfhound*

How long is an elephant pregnant?   *2 years*

What is the state with the longest name?
     Rhode Island and Providence Plantations

What president gave a 40 minute speech after being shot in his ribs by a radical in Milwaukee?   *T. Roosevelt*

How many guys does the average girl kiss before getting married?   *65*

How many U.S. Presidents were born in Ohio?   *7*

What is Ohio's state bug?   *Ladybug*

How much did a Model T cost at first?   *$600.00*

What was Harry Truman's middle name?   *S*

What was Abe Lincoln's middle name?   *Didn't have one*

Where is the oldest Republican Club in Ohio?   *Delphos*

Who was our tallest president?   *Lincoln 6'4"*
Bush 6'3"

What are the largest cities in the world population-wise?
1-Tokyo   2-Mexico City   3-New York

What two countries have the largest trade agreement?   *U.S./Canada*

If the world was an hour long, meaning the whole history of the world was an hour long, when in that hour would the dinosaurs come in?
The 59th minute 59th second

What year did the last Civil War veteran die?   *1959 — 117 years old*

What are the biggest cities in Ohio?
   1-Columbus   2-Cleveland   3-Cincinnati

How much does a Lamborghini cost?   *$211,000*

What is the world's biggest animal?   *Blue Whale*

Who were the highest paid athletes in the U.S. in 1990?
   1-Mike Tyson   2-Sugar Ray Leonard   3-Buster Douglas

What was our first national bird?   *Turkey*

What is the world's biggest snake?   *Anaconda*

What is the strongest muscle in the body?   *Tongue*

What part of the body has the most muscles?   *Lips — over 200 muscles*

What are the #1 selling cars in the U.S.?   *Ford Taurus and Honda Accord*

What is the #1 selling war movie?   *Top Gun*

What is the most ever sold video cassette movie?   *E.T.*

Who has the eighth biggest economy in the world?   *California*

What is the main poison in alcohol?   *Ether*

What is the #1 sold food in the U.S.?   *Pizza*

What percent of people in the country are farmers?   *3%*
What percent in the Soviet Union are farmers?   *80%*

What are the top selling soda pops in U.S.?
    1-Coca Cola   2-Pepsi   3-Diet Coke

Where is the biggest college football stadium in the U.S.?
    Ann Arbor, Michigan

How many times has the U.S. used military action since Vietnam?   *22*

The U.S. has used military action around the world approximately 200 times.
Out of these times how many has Congress declared an Act of War?
    5 times: WWI, WWII, Spanish-American War, War of 1812, Mexican War

What are the biggest bears in the world?
Alaskan Brown Bear, Polar Bear, Grizzly Bear

What is the #1 killer of teenagers in this country?   *Drunk driving*

What is the #2 killer of teenagers in this country?   *Suicide*

What are the four largest countries in the world in land size?
1-Soviet Union   2-China   3-Canada   4-United States

What are the four largest countries in the world in population?
1-China   2-India   3-Soviet Union   4-United States

What is the smallest country in the world?   *The Vatican City*

What percent of their time do Americans spend in front of the television?
    40%

Where was the banana split invented?   *Columbus, Ohio*

Where was the United States' first stop light put up?   *Cleveland, Ohio*

Where was the nation's first gas station opened?   *Columbus, Ohio*

Where was the nation's first kindergarten established?   *Columbus, Ohio*

Where was the first Miss America from?   *Columbus, Ohio*

What city had the first drive-in bank?   *Columbus, Ohio*

What are the top selling beers in the United States?
    1-Budweiser   2-Miller Lite   3-Coors Lite

What states have the largest populations?
California, New York, then Texas

What states have the lowest populations?
Alaska, Wyoming, then Vermont

What are the top three states in land area?
Alaska, Texas, then California

What is Ohio's state song?   *"Beautiful Ohio"*

What is Ohio's state motto?   *"All things are possible with God"*

What president served the shortest term?   *William Henry Harrison, 31 days*

What is the smallest state in land area?   *Rhode Island*

Who has the best standard of living in this country?
   1-Asians   2-Whites   3-Mexicans   4-Blacks

What is the biggest corporation in the world?   *Exxon*

What drink do Americans drink more of than any other?   *Milk*

What is the world's smallest bird?   *Hummingbird*

What is the world's largest bird?   *Ostrich*

What is the world's most popular sport?   *Soccer*

What country owns more American property than any other country?
   Great Britain

What is the #1 selling album?   **Thriller** *by Michael Jackson*

What are the top selling singles?
    1-"We Are The World"   2-"Wild Thing"

What is Ronald Reagan's middle name?   *Wilson*

What was the first city in Ohio?   *Marietta*

How many counties are located in Ohio?   *88*

Where was the first professional football team from?   *Canton, Ohio*

What is the world's biggest moving vehicle?   *Oil Tanker*

In what state was it legal (until 1990) to have marijuana in your home?
    Alaska, but less than 4 ounces only

Is there more excise tax on a diamond necklace or a can of beer?
    A can of beer

What are the most common last names in the United States?
   1-Smith (2.5 million)   2-Johnson   3-Williams   4-Brown

What are the most popular dogs in the world?
   1-Poodle   2-German Shepherd

What animal in the world lives longest?   Tortoise

What are the fastest land animals?
   1-Cheetah (70 mph)   2-Gazelle (50 mph)   3-Race Horses and Jack
   Rabbits (45 mph)

What are the fastest animals in water?
   1-Barracuda/Sailfish (30 mph)   2-Dolphin (25 mph)   3-Whale (20 mph)

What are the fastest animals in the air?
   1-Hawk (250 mph)   2-Golden Eagle (120 mph)   3-Duck (70 mph)

What are the three most intelligent animals next to man?
    1-Ape   2-Dolphin   3-Pig

What are the world's oldest professions?
    1-Medicine Man (Shaman)   2-Prostitute

What are the three most popular dishes in the U.S.?
    1-Fried Chicken   2-Roast Beef   3-Spaghetti

What are the top three causes of death in the U.S.?
    1-Heart Disease   2-Cancer   3-Stroke

What are the top three worst human fears?
    1-Speaking before a group   2-Heights   3-Insects (Spiders)

What musicians or groups have sold the most albums?
    1-Elvis Presley   2-Beatles   3-The Rolling Stones

Which city is larger in population, Columbus or Denver?   *Columbus*
Which is larger, Columbus or Milwaukee?   *Columbus*

What are the most popular types of ethnic restaurants in the United States?
     1-Chinese   2-Italian   3-Mexican   4-French

Where is the one place in the world that more hot dogs are sold than any-where else?   *O'Hare Airport — 2 million per year*

What are the top five selling candies in the United States?
     1-Snickers   2-Reese's Peanut Butter Cups   3-Peanut M&M's
     4-Plain M&M's   5-Kit Kat

What are the most popular months for television?   *January and February*

What is the least popular month for television?   *July*

In elections in the 1990s, what countries had the top percent of voters turnout?
   1-Czechoslovakia   2-Romania   3-Nicaragua   4-United States

What is the most common illness in the U.S.?   *Common cold*

What are the top ten money-making food restaurants in the U.S.?
   1-McDonald's   2-Burger King   3-K.F.C. 4-Pizza Hut
   5-Hardee's/Roy Rogers   6-Wendy's   7-Domino's Pizza
   8-Dairy Queen   9-Taco Bell   10-Arby's

What are the four biggest money-making department stores in the U.S.?
   1-Sears   2-Wal-Mart   3-K-Mart   4-Dayton-Hudson

What is the biggest department store as far as size?   *Macy's in New York*

How much does the average man sweat a day?   *2 gallons*

What job in the U.S. employs more women most frequently?   *Bank teller*

What is the number one form of birth control in the U.S.?   *Sterilization*

What state has the highest percent of students graduating from high school?   *Minnesota — 89%*

What state has the lowest percent?   *Louisiana — 61%*

What are the top conversation topics people talk about?
   1-Weather   2-Sports

What are the top snack foods sold in America?
   *1-Potato Chips   2-Tortilla Chips   3-Snack Nuts   4-Pretzels
   5-Popcorn*

Where is the biggest McDonald's located?   *Moscow* (two stories)

Where is the biggest K.F.C. located?   *China*

What are the longest running television programs?
   *1-Meet The Press (1947)   2-CBS Evening News (1948)   3-Today (1952)
   4-The Guiding Light (1952)   5-Face The Nation (1959)*

Average American work week: *37.4 hours*
USSR work week: *39 hours*

Average American commute to work: *22 minutes*
USSR commute to work: *63 minutes*

Average American life span: *74.9 years*
USSR life span: *68.9 years*

Percent of American households with cars: *85%*
USSR households with cars: *18%*

Percent of American households with televisions: *93%*
USSR households with televisions: *26%*

Brand names that have become words:
    1-Aspirin 2-Jacuzzi 3-Corn Flakes 4-Dry Ice 5-Escalator 6-Kerosene
    7-Nylon 8-Thermos 9-Trampoline 10-Yo-Yo 11-Zipper 12-Linoleum
    13-Cube Steak 14-Raisin Bran 15-Cellophane

What is the number one pet of Americans?   *Cat*

What is the number one health problem in America?   *Overweight*

What state had the most forms of legal gambling?   *Iowa*

What are the most owned electrical appliances Americans have in their homes?
*1-Television   2-VCR   3-Answering machine   4-Cordless phone
5-Personal computer   6-Compact disc player   7-Camcorder*

What are the three biggest cities in the USSR?
1-Moscow   2-Leningrad   3-Kiev

The most popular spectator sports in the U.S. are?
1-Thoroughbred racing   2-Baseball   3-Greyhound racing

Seven most popular natural attractions visited in the U.S.:
>   1-Grand Canyon   2-Yellowstone National Park   3-Niagara Falls
>   4-Mt. McKinley, Alaska   5-California's Redwood Trees   6-Florida
>   Everglades

Ten biggest cities in the U.S. by population:
>   1-New York   2-Los Angeles   3-Chicago   4-Houston
>   5-Philadelphia   6-San Diego   7-Detroit   8-Dallas   9-Phoenix
>   10-San Antonio

What are the top ten most common jobs of teenagers in the summer?
>   1-Babysitter   2-Janitorial cleaner   3-Grounds keeper   4-Farm
>   helper   5-Gas station attendant   6-Retail store helper   7-Cashier
>   8-Retail sales person   9-Waiter/Waitress   10-Cook

What are the subjects people take pictures of most?
>   1-Family celebrations   2-People they know   3-Children
>   4-Travel/Vacation   5-Outdoor scenes   6-Animals/Pets

What are the three largest hotel chains in the U.S. by size?
>   1-Holiday Inn   2-Best Western   3-Days Inn

What are the five top reasons Americans give for being late to work?
*1-Traffic   2-Oversleeping   3-Procrastination   4-Duties at home
5-Car trouble*

Who are the top female singers with the most gold albums (million dollar sellers)?   *1-Barbra Streisand   2-Linda Ronstadt   3-Reba McEntire
4-Olivia Newton-John   5-Dolly Parton*

Who are the three winningest teams on Monday Night Football?
1-LA Raiders   2-San Francisco 49ers   3-Miami Dolphins

What are the top two tourist attractions in Ohio?
1-Amish Country (4 million a year)   2-Cedar Point (3 million a year)

What three countries do Americans travel to most?
1-Mexico   2-Canada   3-England

THE lips contain more muscles than any part of the body. Some psychologists say that if you want to know what a person is thinking read his lips, not his eyes.

Empire State Building

100 tons of trash taken out weekly.
14 people died when constructing it.
1945 a plane crashed into it killing 14 (79th floor).
Winds move it 2 inches.

LUDWIG van Beethoven was completely deaf when he wrote his last symphony.

IDI Amin, the former terrorist leader of Uganda, used to torture people by tying them down and placing a wild sewer rat on their stomachs. He then would place a hot boiling pot of water on the rat. The rat, going crazy and having nowhere to go, would eat his way through the man's stomach and come out his back.

THERE are parts of the Amazon River, the largest river in the world, that you can not see across.

SCIENTISTS predict that every home contains 30,000 spiders.

A No. 2 pencil can draw a line 70 miles long.

A giant sequoia in California nicknamed "The General Sherman" measures 272 feet in the air and 79 feet in circumference. Mathematicians have calculated that if it were cut down there would be enough wood to build 35 homes.

THE theme park with the most rides in the world is Cedar Point in Sandusky, Ohio.

IF a farmer pulls a horse out of a burning barn and then lets go, the horse will run back into the inflamed barn.

FAMOUS inventor Guglielmo Marconi was once admitted to a psychiatric hospital by his friends for talking about a method he had found to transmit messages through the air. He later went on to develop wireless telegraphy for radio broadcasting.

IN 1850 machines in the U.S. did 35% of the work, people did 13% and animals did 52%. Of all the work today, machines do 98% of the work, people 1% and animals less than 1%.

BEFORE comic singer Weird Al Yankovic became famous, he was turned down on an audition for *The Gong Show*.

EIGHTY percent of all food on a salad bar has been either touched, coughed or sneezed on.

THERE should be a stop light for every thousand people in your town.

WHEN a beaver's dam breaks, other beavers will come from miles around to help rebuild it. Beavers also make themselves a clean bed to sleep on daily.

THE ordinary Japanese worker spends an average of ten hours at his job. Afterwards, he accompanies his boss to a local pub for a few hours, making his usual work day 10-14 hours five to six days per week. Some pre-schools in Japan have the young students attend in just their underwear, teaching them to adapt to the physical struggles in the world as well as challenging them mentally.

A survey taken in the '80s asked Americans if it were possible what president they would have as president again from Carter on back. The most picked president was Harry Truman.

A chimpanzee is four times stronger than a man.

1914 — Hollywood motion picture company signed a contract with Mexican leader Pancho Villa for $25,000. The director told Pancho how and where to fight. The director made Pancho start fighting every morning at 9:00 a.m. When the film was brought back to Hollywood it was found to be unbelievable and most of it had to be reshot.

1890 — Emperor Menelik, the former leader of Abyssinia (Ethiopia), ordered three electric chairs from an American manufacturer after learning of their use in New York's Auburn Prison. After they arrived he found out they would not work: Abyssinia had no electricity. He used one chair for a throne.

Famous People And Their Prior Jobs

Carol Burnett	Usher
Johnny Carson	Magician
Perry Como	Barber
Sean Connery	Truck Driver
Albert Einstein	Patent Office Clerk
Bob Hope	Boxer
Golda Meir	Teacher
Marilyn Monroe	Factory Worker
Elvis Presley	Truck Driver
Babe Ruth	Bartender

High School Drop-Outs

Cher	Steve McQueen
Henry Ford	Al Pacino
George Gershwin	Frank Sinatra
Adolf Hitler	Orville and Wilbur Wright
Dean Martin	

I worked for Governor Voinovich beginning in 1991. You will never meet a more honest man. His main goal was to do one thing: Make Ohio a better place to live for us and future generations. Governor Voinovich had a philosophy that if you do what you are doing right now the best that you can, the future will take care of itself.

I am a Jack Kemp supporter and believe he could be a great president. I met with him in Columbus, Ohio.

I presented Phyllis Diller a proclamation on behalf of Governor Voinovich when she did a fund-raiser for Bluffton College. With me is my wife, Lori. Phyllis spreads so much cheer wherever she goes.

You will never meet a man who loves his family more than John Cooper, coach of the Buckeyes. I had a meeting with him at his office. He has that Buckeye tenacity that makes him never give up.